LET'S TALK ABOUT

I0558813

ELEVATING CONNECTIONS TO COMMUNITY:

Mastering the CSA Methodology for Professionals

CLAY HICKS

Infinite Impressions Publishing
610 Harpwood Dr.
Franklin, OH 45005
www.InfiniteImpressionsPublishing.com

ISBN: 979-8-9908008-1-6

What is C.S.A. ?

The Connect, Serve, and Ask™ (C.S.A.) one-to-one methodology supports professionals seeking a comprehensive understanding of a proven approach that transcends within your professional endeavors. By embracing the Connect, Serve, and Ask™ mindset and strategy in your one-to-ones with others, you will not only gain valuable insights from those you're meeting with but also play a pivotal role in nurturing a culture of trust and collaboration. Through active listening, demonstrating empathy, and consistently fulfilling commitments, you pave the way for meaningful connections and collective advancement.

Connect, Serve, and Ask™ is designed for individuals eager to grasp a proven strategy and delves deep into the core principles for success in your Word-of-Mouth Marketing Strategy.

Embracing the Connect, Serve, and Ask™ mindset in practical one-to-one scenarios, you'll not only unlock valuable insights but also actively contribute to fostering a culture of trust and collaboration within your community.

Chapter
1

Connect Your Way to Success

These questions formed a valuable framework for each interaction:

- Where are you from?
- What's your personal story?
- What do you do professionally?
- Tell me about your family.
- What are your hobbies?

These connecting questions transformed my one-to-one meetings, allowing relationships to deepen and genuine connections to form more organically. As the conversations became richer and the bonds stronger, I realized that building rapport was crucial before any meaningful service could be offered. It took another 500-plus meetings for me to internalize a vital lesson: Connecting authentically is the first step; serving effectively comes next.

I learned that true service extends beyond a mere exchange of favors or networking opportunities—it's about understanding and empathy. Unless the individuals I met felt a genuine connection and trusted in the relationship, they weren't likely to open up and engage in a mutually vulnerable and beneficial manner. This realization reshaped my approach to professional and personal interactions, reinforcing the importance of connecting first and serving second. Through this approach, not only did I grow as a connector, but I also enhanced my ability to positively impact others' lives in meaningful ways.

Thus, as I moved forward, my mission evolved. It wasn't just about connecting for the sake of personal or professional gain but about building a legacy of interconnectedness that champions cooperation and collective empowerment.

Through this transformative process, I also discovered the subtleties involved in maintaining these connections. It wasn't merely about initial encounters; it was equally about nurturing those connections to foster long-term relationships and networks. The profound interactions didn't end after the meetings; follow-ups were crucial. I began to invest time in sending personalized messages, recalling specific details from our conversations, and checking in on the progress of their personal and professional endeavors.

Reflecting on this journey, I realized that each interaction was a step toward mastering the art of connection. The role of empathy, active listening, and genuine curiosity became the cornerstones of my interactions. They were not just strategies but became integral parts of who I am, enhancing how I engage with the world around me.

My aim is not only to create links but to weave a resilient, empathetic network that thrives on shared successes and collaborative achievements. In doing so, I strive to inspire others to embrace connection not merely as a skill but as a vital component of human experience, driving positive change and deeper societal impact.

My Word-of-Mouth Marketing Journey began with CONNECT.

Action Steps to Connect your Way to Success:

1. **Connecting to Serve:** Before engaging in dialogue with other professionals, it's crucial to dedicate effort towards researching and comprehensively understanding their backgrounds, professional fields, and interests.

2. **Active Listen:** Active listening is an essential skill that demands your undivided attention to the individual you are engaging with in conversation. To truly practice active listening, it is crucial to minimize any distractions and maintain eye contact. Listen to not only the words but the inflection in their tone. The meaning behind their words. You'll find that some things they talk about bring more excitement or passion. Those are things you can find commonality with.

3. **Be Relatable:** One compelling strategy to enhance relatability with fellow professionals is to actively seek out common ground or shared experiences during your interactions. Start by exploring similarities in backgrounds, such as educational paths or geographic origins. Delve into common interests like hobbies or passion projects, or align on professional goals and aspirations that resonate with both of you.

Reflection Questions:

1. **Reflect on Connecting to Serve:** How effectively am I preparing for my conversations by researching and understanding the backgrounds, professional fields, and interests of the individuals I connect with? Can I identify specific instances where this preparation directly contributed to a more meaningful and productive conversation?

2. **Reflect on Active Listening:** Am I consistently providing my full attention during conversations without distractions? How well do I listen without preparing my response or interrupting, and how does this impact the depth and quality of the interactions I have?

3. **Reflect on Being Relatable:** To what extent am I successful in finding common ground or shared experiences in my interactions? How have these shared points of connection influenced the relationships and outcomes of my professional engagements? Have I been able to foster a genuine sense of understanding and rapport through personal anecdotes and shared interests?

NOTES:

2

Service Driven Transformative Outcomes

"Serve" embodies the selfless act of putting others' needs and aspirations above our own, facilitating growth, support, and empowerment. It goes beyond mere assistance; it is a committed endeavor to uplift and enhance the lives and environments we touch. At its core, to serve is to enrich and transform, forging deeper human connections and fostering a legacy of generosity and impact.

Serving other professionals fosters a culture of collaboration and mutual respect, creating a network where knowledge, resources, and support are reciprocally exchanged, enhancing collective success. This service-driven approach can elevate career trajectories, as it often leads to opportunities for mentorship, partnerships, and professional growth for both the giver and receiver. Moreover, consistently serving others cultivates a reputation of reliability and generosity, establishing a professional as a respected and influential leader within their industry.

From the outset, my primary aim was to serve others like I had previously stated when discussing Connect. Initially, this simply meant finding ways to be helpful in any situation. After conducting my first 500 one-to-one meetings, I realized there was so much more I could learn about effectively serving others. My understanding deepened significantly by the time I reached my 1,600th meeting, which occurred with a gentleman in Columbus while I was in the process of developing the new H7 Columbus market.

During that time, I was eagerly meeting with any professional willing to connect, but this particular meeting stood out and became a defining moment in my journey. It culminated in the gentleman introducing me to 11 other professionals in Columbus, making it one of the most impactful experiences I had encountered to that point. As I drove home, reflecting on our discussion, a pivotal interaction came to mind. Midway through our 60 minute one-to-one, he unexpectedly asked, "How can I help you?" This question took me by surprise, as it mirrored the way most of my previous interactions concluded.

This encounter prompted a significant shift in my approach. I pondered why he chose to raise this query midway through our one-to-one instead of at the end and what impact it had on the dynamic of our meeting. Inspired by this, I decided to adopt this proactive approach of asking how I could assist others midway through our one-to-one, rather than as a closing remark. I began implementing this practice the very next day, realizing that this method allowed me to serve others more effectively and with greater impact.

This was a monumental turning point; what I initially termed "Add value to others" naturally evolved into what I now simply call "Serve." This strategy not only enhanced my ability to connect but also profoundly deepened the level of assistance I could offer, cementing my commitment to truly serving those around me.

The transformation in my professional interactions taught me the immense value of proactive service. This new approach led to more open, symbiotic exchanges where both parties felt equally heard and valued right from the onset. The strategy soon proved to be universally effective, creating numerous opportunities for deeper collaboration. It wasn't long before I noticed a significant enhancement in the quality of my professional relationships and an increase in referrals and joint ventures.

The journey of refining this approach was not immediate. It took approximately 900 more individual one-to-ones before I began to identify a set of questions that consistently facilitated deeper, more meaningful conversations. These questions formed a valuable framework for each interaction:

- How can I help you?
- Who would you like to meet?
- Who is your ideal client/industry/type of person?
- How is your business going?
- How can my expertise help?

The concept of "Serve" has become the cornerstone of my professional ethos. It underscores every interaction I engage in, ensuring that each meeting is not just about transactional exchanges but about genuinely understanding and enhancing the lives of those I meet. This philosophy has not only led to sustained professional success but has also allowed me to contribute to a more collaborative and empathetic business landscape. Serving is influential, it supports trust-earning opportunities for both parties, and supports my Word-of-Mouth marketing across the world now.

Action Steps to Service-Driven Transformative Outcomes:

1. **Serve before you Ask:** When partaking in Connect, Serve, and Ask™ (C.S.A.) one-to-one sessions, it's essential to meticulously assess the needs and challenges of the other individual through active listening and targeted questioning. Using the insights gained, you can then offer targeted assistance by sharing knowledge, resources, or connections that directly respond to their unique challenges.

2. **Be of Service to Others:** When endeavoring to foster trusted relationships through Connect, Serve, and Ask™ (C.S.A.) one-to-ones, it is imperative to provide assistance, resources, or connections tailored to align with the other person's specific needs and aspirations. Sharing our expertise, experiences, or insights plays a vital role in helping them navigate and surmount the challenges they encounter.

3. **Follow-Through:** To enhance effectiveness and

ensure mutual accountability during Connect, Serve, and Ask™ (C.S.A.) one-to-ones, it is essential to clearly define and agree upon specific action steps that both participants will undertake. These action steps must be realistic, attainable, and measurable, effectively paving the way for tangible success.

Reflection Questions:

1. **Reflect on Serve before you Ask:** How effectively am I employing active listening and targeted questioning to truly understand the unique needs and challenges of my counterparts in C.S.A. one-to-one sessions? Am I navigating these discussions in a way that allows me to offer highly specific assistance tailored to their needs, thereby establishing a robust foundation of trust?

2. **Reflect on Being of Service to Others:** In what ways am I demonstrating genuine commitment and care in my interactions? How well am I leveraging my expertise to identify and seize opportunities that add significant value to others, and what impact has this approach had on strengthening the professional relationships I am building?

3. **Reflect on Follow-Through:** How successful am I in clearly defining and documenting agreed-upon action steps during C.S.A. one-to-one sessions? Am I ensuring these steps are realistic, attainable, and measurable, and how effective is my follow-up process in promoting mutual accountability and driving progress towards our shared goals?

NOTES:

Chapter

3

Activate Your Ask

Asking others for help with introductions to their prospects can significantly expand your professional network, opening doors to new opportunities and collaborations that might otherwise remain inaccessible. This practice demonstrates your proactive nature and willingness to leverage existing relationships, which can enhance your reputation as a connected and resourceful professional. Additionally, it deepens trust and reciprocity within your professional circles. Engaging others for introductions encourages a collaborative atmosphere where mutual support is valued and practiced.

The practice of the ASK, particularly for introductions, marks the pivotal final step in the Connect, Serve, and Ask™ (C.S.A.) methodology. This is a strategy that took shape after I engaged in nearly 2,500 one-to-one meetings with various professionals. The significance of this step became clear to me during a transformative period in the winter of 2018, which was a bustling time when I was actively meeting with professionals and diligently working to expand my network.

As I navigated through numerous one-to-ones, a period of introspection made me realize a critical missing element in my approach: I wasn't genuinely asking for help. Up until then, my focus during these meetings was primarily on serving others' needs and ensuring that the professionals I introduced were well taken care of.

This one-way approach to networking illuminated a stark reality—I was inadvertently neglecting my own professional needs by not leveraging these opportunities to ask for introductions in return. Each time someone asked whom I wanted to meet, I responded almost out of reflex, downplaying my own needs, as if to suggest that everything was fine and I didn't require any assistance. However, the reality was quite different; I wasn't receiving any introductions, which was stunting my potential for broader network growth.

The realization hit me profoundly, like a ton of bricks; was I too egotistical to admit my need for help? Did I somehow believe that asking for assistance diminished my professional stature? These introspections led me to understand that not only was it acceptable to ask for help, but it was also necessary and expected. I owed it to myself to seize every opportunity to advocate for my professional needs just as vigorously as I supported others to do.

Driven by this newfound perspective, I seriously began to adjust my strategy. By August 2018, after reflecting on my experiences and distilling the essence of my interactions, the formalized concept of Connect, Serve, and Ask™ officially took shape. This holistic approach not only focused on making thoughtful connections and earnestly serving others but also embraced the crucial aspect of asking—a mutual exchange that enhances the value of networks for all involved.

The evolution of the Connect, Serve, and Ask™ framework was a crucial development in my professional journey, with the ASK playing an integral role in shaping a more balanced, effective, and reciprocal networking strategy. It transformed how I approach professional relationships, emphasizing that while serving is noble, asking is equally essential for mutual growth and success.

Action Steps: B2B

In the world of B2B (Business-to-Business) networking and relationship-building, the art of asking for introductions or referrals can be a game-changer. As a B2B professional, you understand the power and potential that lies within a well-connected network. However, the key to maximizing the benefits of networking lies not just in asking for introductions, but in asking for them in a specific and targeted manner.

B2B Professional: B2B stands for Business-to-Business sales

When it comes to seeking introductions or referrals, one strategy that can greatly enhance your success is to ask specifically for industries or companies. Instead of vaguely asking for general introductions, specifically target industries or companies that align with your professional goals and objectives.

Reflection Questions:

1. **Reflect on Clarity:** How clear and specific am I in communicating my own professional needs when I ask for help or introductions? Am I articulating what types of connections would be most beneficial to my growth and why?

2. **Reflect on Pride:** Am I allowing my pride or concerns about appearing needy to hinder my ability to ask effectively in professional settings? How can I overcome these feelings to foster a culture of mutual support and reciprocity in my network?

3. **Reflect on Balance:** Do I regularly reflect on the balance of giving and receiving within my professional relationships? How can I ensure that I am not only providing value to others but also openly expressing and addressing my own needs through these interactions?

Conclusion:

The Connect, Serve, and Ask™ (C.S.A.) methodology fundamentally transforms word-of-mouth marketing by cultivating strong, reciprocal relationships that propel professional success.

Starting with 'Connect', this approach prioritizes genuine engagement, allowing professionals to understand and align with the goals and challenges of their contacts. Following up with 'Serve', individuals demonstrate commitment by actively contributing to the success of others, thereby deepening trust and

Action Steps: B2C

In the realm of B2C (Business-to-Consumer) networking and relationship-building, the art of asking for introductions or referrals can be a game-changer for the growth and success of a B2C professional. Building connections with the right people can open doors to new customers, partnerships, and opportunities. However, it's not just about asking for any introductions or referrals; it's about asking specifically for "types of people". This communication strategy can significantly enhance a B2C professional's effectiveness in expanding their network and reaching their target audience.

B2C Professional: B2C stands for Business-to-Consumer sales

When it comes to seeking introductions or referrals, asking for specific types of people can be invaluable. Instead of simply requesting general connections, the focus shifts to identifying and attracting individuals who fit a particular profile or have specific characteristics that align with the B2C professional's target audience.

NOTES:

establishing credibility. The final step, 'Ask', encourages clear communication of personal needs, inviting contacts to provide support that further enriches mutual understanding and cooperation.

Implementing C.S.A. into daily professional interactions not only magnifies the quantity of referrals and introductions you receive but also significantly enhances their quality. This method fosters a vibrant network where support flows freely, multiplying each participant's reach and impact. As C.S.A. embeds the principles of empathy, generosity, and clarity into the fabric of your professional engagements, it constructs a dynamic ecosystem conducive to sustained growth and success.

I urge professionals keen on maximizing their word-of-mouth marketing effectiveness to embrace and practice the Connect, Serve, and Ask™ methodology. By doing so, you set the stage for a thriving career enriched by meaningful and productive professional relationships.

NOTES:

www.ingramcontent.com/pod-product-compliance
Lightning Source LLC
Chambersburg PA
CBHW070812120626
46557CB00002B/834